For too long, our society has shrugged off bullying by labeling it a 'rite of passage' and by asking students to simply 'get over it.' Those attitudes need to change. Every day, students are bullied into silence and are afraid to speak up. Let's break this silence and end school bullying.

Linda Sanchez

I TOLD MY KID TO
FIGHT BACK

Examining Generational
Differences Between Bullying
YESTERDAY
and
TODAY

MONICA
MCLAURINE

I Told My Kid To Fight Back: Examining Generational
Differences Between Bullying Yesterday and Today.

For information contact: MRenee Enterprise Inc.
P.O. Box 694
LaVergne, TN 37086

Printed in the United States of America

ISBN: 978-0-692-10804-8

LCCN: 2018908277

In Loving Memory
Of
My Loving Father

Larry Thomas McLaurine

December 2, 1950-November 18, 2015

My forever Supporter, I miss you Daddy

Monica

Thank You…

As always, thank you to my Lord and Savior for entrusting me with this message to the world. I must admit this assignment has been very challenging and at times I questioned my ability to write this message.

God has truly placed some real-life Angels in my path to help keep me focused and on task in order to complete this assignment. The support from my Mommy Jean McLaurine, my brother Reggie, my sister-in-law Na Tasha and the rest of my family has been immeasurable. Your love and encouragement mean the world to me and I would be lost without you.

To my countless friends and extended family that have offered to help me, answered my questions, encouraged me and to my writing session partner LaNessa…..thank you. To those that checked in with me to make sure spent time on this book every day and those of you that prayed for me and offered your assistance…..thank you.

Last but not least, a huge thank you to the readers of this book. I appreciate you giving me a chance to express my heart and my mind on a very touchy subject. My prayer is that it will be worth your time.

Monica

Table of Contents

<u>Preface</u>

We all know that bullying is a very touchy subject. I get that. I also know that we want our children to be safe as possible. I get it. I am writing this book to challenge our current way of thinking. Usually when we hear of someone being bullied, it is very common to hear "That kid should have fought back!" "Kids now days are little such little wimps!" "Kids need to toughen up!" Then you will always hear this one statement... "When I was a kid we used to…." This statement is the one that has led me to write this book.

My intention is not to question the way you counsel your children on the issue of bullying or anything of that nature. My intent is to spotlight the other side of this issue.

Oftentimes we as adults don't consider how bullying has changed dramatically over the years. With the inception of the internet, social media and text messaging, bullying has transformed to a completely level. My greatest hope is that you will read this book with an open mind and really think before you tell your child to fight back.

<u>What They Said...</u>

While I was doing research for this book, I was blessed with the opportunity to sit down with a group of young people to discuss the topic of my book. To my surprise, over all they were excited about it. They also gave me some great information and reaffirmed why I am writing this book.

I am going to share with you some of their concerns and hopefully, address some of their concerns with this book. My prayer is that somethings I am placing in this book will help open conversations between parents and their kids.

It may seem like the following topics may not be specific to bullying but they are related. They all will show barriers to communication between parent and child. We have to be able to communicate effectively in order to get a handle on bullying. Prayerfully, this section can aid in bridging the conversation gap.

First they shared with me is that they feel like their parents can't relate to what they are going through. They told me that if they do tell them about their problems (bullying included), they tell them to handle things like they did when they were young. They felt like they didn't understand that things are not the same as they were when their parents were young. They feel like it is sometimes useless to talk with their parents because of this. They found it difficult to get their parents to see the situation from their perspective. That makes them hesitant to share with their parents when something may be happening to them. How their parents handled a particular situation is not necessarily how their child would handle things the same way.

Second they told me they feel like when they share their issues with their parents, their feelings/concerns are minimized and are not taken seriously. One young lady told me that she told her mom that she was depressed and her mother replied that "she was too young to be depressed." Others chimed in with their own stories, but they all felt like, at times, their feelings were minimized when they shared their feelings with their parents. It was explained that when they are made to feel this way, they tend not to want to open up to their parents. They are looking for support in that moment and unfortunately, they don't feel like they received it.

Thirdly, I was told when they come to their parents to vent about what they are going through, they are told how to handle the problem when they only want their parents to listen. It is natural for parents to want to solve the problems your child may be experiencing. However, your children may need you to listen and not always try to fix it. They would like to at least try to solve it themselves before getting to your help. Sometimes they can fix it themselves and sometimes they can't. Either way they would like to try. Sometimes they are just looking for a supportive ear and to reinforce that you are there for them and always will be.

By no means do I believe that any parent would intentionally dismiss or minimize their kid's feelings or needs. These are the perceptions that kids have based upon their parents' responses. Based upon these perceptions,

Communication lines between parent and child may become damaged. This is something that should not be jeopardized or taken lightly. Open communication between parent and child are imperative to assist their child with issues including bullying.

Prayerfully, I hope this book can start open and healthy communication on this ever present issue.

Just To Make Sure

We Are On The

Same Page……

Chapter One

Definition of Bullying and Bullying Types

Definition of Bullying

When you think of what the definition of bullying, it is never really cut and dry. If you were to ask someone what it means, they will talk about the types of bullying rather than the actual definition.

Merriam-Webster Dictionary defines Bullying as: blustering, browbeating person; *especially*: one who is habitually cruel, insulting, or threatening to others who are weaker, smaller, or in some way vulnerable. Stopbullying.com also defines bullying as: Bullying is unwanted, aggressive behavior among school aged children that involves a real or perceived power imbalance. The behavior is repeated, or has the potential to be repeated, over time. Both kids who are bullied and who bully others may have serious, lasting problems. That latter definition is what I tend to use the most in my presentations and workshops.

This definition reminds me of myself. I too was bullied as a child. The last sentence in this paragraph was a description of my life. The remnants of the verbal and emotional bullying I received affected me well into my adulthood because I never dealt with the pain I felt when I was bullied. Traces of those unresolved feelings turned into insecurities that influenced how I conducted myself throughout my life. The types of clothes I bought, the shoes I wore, the relationships I involved myself in all stemmed from my childhood bullying experiences.

Four types of Bullying:

Physical: Physical Bullying. This is any bullying that hurts someone's body or damages their possessions. Stealing, shoving, hitting, fighting, and destroying property all are types of physical bullying. Physical bullying is rarely the first form of bullying that a target will experience. (Source: respect@all.org)

Emotional/Verbal: Emotional bullying isn't just seen on the playground; emotional bullying, although likely subtler, is seen in adult relationships and workplaces too. An emotional bully might: (source: healthyplace.com)

- Name-call, tease or mock
- Use sarcasm
- Threaten
- Put-down or belittle
- Lie

☐ Humiliate others

<u>Social Alienation:</u> is defined as when a bully intentionally excludes another individual from a specific social group or group of mutual friends with the intention to hurt or embarrass others. This is one of the most misunderstood forms of bullying, so let me take a little time to further explain it.

When your child goes to lunch to school, who do they sit with? When they go to recess, who do they interact with? When they are walking home from school, who do they usually walk with? Most often during adolescent years, your child's friends are some of the most important people in their lives. They are with them all day and on the phone with each other when they are apart. Imagine in one without warning, that all changes. Your kid's friends no longer wants to talk to them or eat lunch with them. They start spreading rumors (whether true or untrue) about your child and now everyone is upset with him or her. Kids have the right to be friends or hang out with whomever they choose. They also are free to choose when they no longer want to be friends with anyone. However, when they deliberately isolate someone from another person on group to intentionally hurt them or shame them, turns into social alienation. They do not have the right to create a hostile environment for others. Kids who participate in these scenarios can be relentless and can create aggressive situations. These actions have the potential to escalate and create unsafe environments.

Cyberbullying: is bullying that takes place using electronic technology. Electronic technology includes devices and equipment such as cell phones, computers, and tablets as well as communication tools including social media sites,

text messages, chat, and websites.

Chapter Two

Bullying In Past Generations

<u>Ask Yourself….</u>

1. **Describe your first encounter with a bully?**

2. **How old were you?**

3. **How did it make you feel?**

Bullying in Previous Years

Bullying has been around, in some shape or fashion, for years. **Most** of us were encouraged to handle bullying pretty much the same way. "You have to "stand up to them", or fight your bully back." "You have to stick up for yourself, or they will never leave you alone!" "Get back out there and fight them!" It has been said that this is the only way to handle a bully. We all hoped that whoever was getting bullied would triumphantly get the best of the bully, and the bully would know to never try to bully them ever again. Yes, there were times when this scenario would play out exactly like this. The bullied would become strong and no longer the victim. The only thing is we often forget about the other possible outcomes. Here are some things I would like for you to think about. This is what bullying looked like when we were coming up.

~Disclaimer~

After an exhaustive search to find statistical data relating to bullying before the year 2000, it has been relatively fruitless. Prior to the 1970's, a diminutive amount of data, and/or research, was conducted before Dan Olweus, the author of *Aggression in the Schools: Bullies and Whipping Boys* was published. Here is some of the data I was able to find.

What the Studies Say 1970's -1990's

During the 1950's through the early 1990's bullying looked different than it does today... Kids that were usually the target of bullies had one or more of the following characteristics:

- New kid on the block
- Smallest in class

- Timid

- Lacked self-esteem

- Less-likely to fight back

- Religious

- Poor and/or rich

- Fat and/or thin

- Suffered with extreme acne, wore braces, glasses, or had a disability

- Race and/or ethnicity that could be viewed as inferior to the bully

Common reactions to being bullied:

- Withdrawn

- Sad

- Angry

- Become a bully

Methods of Bullying

- In-person

- Over the phone

Provis, Steven Arthur, "Bullying (1950 - 2010): The Bully and the Bullied" (2012). *Dissertations.* Paper 381.

http://ecommons.luc.edu/luc_diss/381

Suicides and Attempted Suicides attributed to Bullying

I was unable to locate concrete statistics and percentages on suicides, and attempted suicides, related to bullying during the years of 1950-2000. However, here is what I was able to find:

☐ Kelly Yeomans (May 1984 - September 1997) committed suicide (overdose of painkillers) due to continuous bullying.

☐ Hamed Bismel Nastoh (December 1985 - March 11, 2000) committed suicide (jumped from a bridge) due to continuous bullying.

☐ Dawn Marie-Wesley (May 1986 - November 2000) committed suicide (hung herself) due to continuous bullying.

• Greg Barrett (Gay was his last name originally but he legally had it changed) gave a detailed account of his bullying experience while in junior high school in 1983 at a school board meeting in Houston, Texas. After receiving little to no help when he reported his experience to teachers and the principal, he went home and contemplated suicide. He said he in his house, found his father's 45-caliber gun and placed it in his mouth. Thankfully, he did not follow through with his original plan of committing suicide. Later, in that same meeting, he accused the Houston area school superintendent of being his bully. The superintendent denied those claims.

<u>**Stories**</u>

<u>**of**</u>

<u>**Those Who Were Bullied: 1970's -2000's**</u>

I have conducted bullying workshops across the country and have had the opportunity to talk to bullying survivors of all ages, races, and gender. Their individual stories may differ slightly, but are all centered around similar instances.

One day while thinking about my book and its contents, I was led to poll my Facebook followers. I asked the following questions "Were you bullied in school? If so, how did you handle it?" The responses I received were golden and I was pleasantly surprised by the number of candid and vivid responses.

I received the expected answers such as, "No", I have never been bullied". Then I also received the triumphant responses, "Yeah I was bullied, but I beat her up so she left me alone." This is the answer that everyone loves and wants to hear. This is the ideal outcome that we would all like to see happen when dealing with bullies. We want to see the bullies get dealt with accordingly. Unfortunately, this is not always the case.

One category with a big response was from individuals that were bullied, but never did anything about it. Either they shrugged it off, kept it to themselves, or were too afraid do so anything about it. This is the group I was unfortunately a part of. I was bullied for years and never mentioned it to anyone. I figured if I just ignored it, it would eventually stop. I never wanted to tell my parents, or my teachers. I felt that "telling" on my bullies could, and would, make my situation worse. So I held on to the hurt and shame for years, and buried it as if it never happened.

I also didn't want to show any emotion I didn't want to show them, or give them the satisfaction of knowing that they hurt me. I remember once being at church for choir rehearsal, and I had on a knock-off jacket that was similar to a very popular brand name. There was a particular young lady also in the choir that had parents, and a grandmother, that bought her all the name brand items she wanted and she always wore them proudly. I remember sitting there with the rest of the choir and she began to talk about my jacket. She stated how it was a fake, and other mean and hurtful things. I was embarrassed and hurt by what she said, but I didn't let my hurt show. I felt that if I cried it would only give her more ammunition to use against me. I acted as if it never fazed me, but deep down, this instant and others like it, caused more damage than I realized. When I finally acknowledged that it happened, I was finally able to move on from those past hurts. I pray others have done, or will do, this as well.

Another large response category was that people who had reached their limit and lashed out against their bully. Some also admitted that in trying to defend themselves they turned into a bully themselves. Others spoke about confronting their bullies, or preparing to finally fight them. One person mentioned when she confronted her bully, a teacher intervened and stopped it that before anything happened between her and her bully. She referred to it as a divine intervention. When I first read her response, it tickled me, but I could also relate to her sense of relief due to her teacher's actions.

One particular story stuck out to me because of the individual's vivid recollection of her "fed up moment". She recalled her story like it had just happened to her yesterday. Here is what she shared with me:

"Yes, I was bullied in the 6th grade. It started on a field trip to see the Ramses exhibit. My friends and I were walking and talking, and this girl bumped into me. I turned told her I was sorry, and started walking away.

She came up to me and told me she was going to "kick my butt after school". I was surprised, but didn't think anything of it until after school. She tried to fight me the entire way home. This led to weeks of her bullying me the entire day, before school, during lunch, at recess and after school. I was terrified of her because she always looked mad, and had her hair cut like Anita Baker before the style was popular. One day I was sitting in my living room and "she" was walking through the courtyard headed towards the Candy Lady's house (every neighborhood had one back then). As I sat there watching her leisurely stroll by I felt a rag building inside me. I jumped up, swung the front door open, and to my own amazement yelled, Hey [insert bully's name] you wanna fight!?" I ran out of my house toward her screaming. She turned around, saw me running and swearing at her, and she ran to the Candy Lady's house in fear. I was ready to face whatever butt whooping she had for me because I was tired of being in fear. She was escorted from the Candy Lady's house by the lady's son. He walked with "her" over to me and he said, "Little lady, I've never seen you act like this before". He was right. I told him what she had been doing to me for weeks and I was tired of it. He made us both apologize and agree to be friends. After that day, "she" and I became friends."

My friend shared with me that was the day she learned to NEVER, EVER fear another person. She said that even today she still doesn't. It was a very valuable lesson she has carried with her since the 6th grade.

Her story gave me chills because I could relate to it. I only wish that I had channeled a piece of her courage. But, her journey was her journey and my journey was mine. It is encouraging that both young ladies were able to put their differences aside and become friends. I really wish more stories had a happy ending, and lessons learned by both parties.

You may be wondering what reliving these moments may have to do with the purpose of this book. I believe it is important to bring you back to those events in time, and prayerfully help you remember how it felt to be in that moment. I want to help you remember the emotions that ran through your body, and the effects it had on you. Sometimes we forget what that felt like. I am hoping it will help you imagine what your child could possibly be feeling if they are being bullied. I hope you can also remember what the culture was like in the years of your youth, and see how it differs from the culture of today. Now, let's take a look at what bullying looks like today.

Chapter Two

<u>Reflection</u>

1. Can you relate to any of response categories? If so, which one(s)?

2.   If you had an experience similar to the two latter response categories, how did it feel to relive your experience?

3.   If you had the chance to have a "do-over" with your response to your bullying experience, what would it be?

Chapter Three

What

Bullying Looks

Like Today

<u>2001-Present Day</u>

<u>Statistics reported on bullying</u>

- 28% of U.S. students in grades 6-12 have experienced bullying.

- 20% of U.S. students in grades 9-12 have experienced bullying.

- 30% (approximately) have admitted to bullying others.

- 70.6% of young people have said they witnessed bullying in their schools with 41% admitting to witnessing bullying once a week or more.

- 49% of children in grades 4-12 reported being bullied in the past year at school at least once.

Stopbullying.gov https://www.stopbullying.gov/media/facts/index.html accessed 20 April 2018

Kids who are usually targets

- Perceived as different from their peers, such as being overweight or underweight, wearing glasses or different clothing, being new to a school, or being unable to afford what their peers consider "cool".
- Perceived as weak, or unable to defend themselves.
- Depressed, anxious, or have low self-esteem.
- Less popular than others and have few friends,
- Doesn't get along well with others, seen as annoying or provoking, or antagonize others for attention.
- LGBTQ

Common reactions to being bullied

- Withdrawn/moody

- Sad

- Angry

- Become a bully

- Self-harm, or attempt self-harm

- Grades start to decline

- Isolates themselves from friends and family

<u>Methods of Bullying</u>

- In-person

- Cell phone/text

- Social Media

- Anonymous websites and applications

- Videos

<u>Suicide and attempted suicide rates attributed to bullying and Cyberbullying</u>

<u>Disclaimer:</u>

Most youth who are involved in bullying do NOT engage in suicide-related behavior. However, it is said that involvement in bullying, along with other risk factors, increases the chances that a young person will engage in suicide-related behaviors.

- Bullied victims are 7% to 9% more likely to consider suicide.

- 20% of youth that are cyberbullied think about suicide.

- Peer victimization in children and adolescents is associated with higher rates of suicidal ideation and suicide attempts.

https://www.meganmeierfoundation.org/statistics.html accessed 26 April 2018
https://nobullying.com/bullying-suicide-statistics/ accessed 26/April 2018

Stories of the Bullied
2001-present

There are countless stories that I could share about young people and bullying. In an effort to make sure the stories are as diverse as possible, I picked out a few stories that hit home to me. In your spare time, I do encourage you to seek out other cases/stories. Unfortunately, with very little effort, you will find plenty of bullying victim stories to choose from.

Joey Kemmerling

While conversing with a friend, Joey, 16, confided in that friend that he was gay. The next day, it seemed as if everyone in the school knew. He recalled being pointed at and laughed at by his classmates. He remembered going into the locker room to change for gym class, and a young man who was standing beside him, gathered his things and moved. He told Joey that he did want him checking him out. Once, he said a teacher asked him if he could "act a little less gay". A student also pulled a knife on Joey and threatened him.

Joey shared that he was very afraid, suffered from nightmares, and also considered taking his own life. In response to his treatment, Joey transferred schools and began to advocate for other students like him.

Rosalie Avila

Rosalie was a 13 year-old girl that was bullied in person, as well as, online. She was taunted by her classmates who made fun of her braces and called her ugly. The bullying she endured lasted for several years.

In late 2017, Rosalie's parents noticed that she was depressed and began to become withdrawn. She was also cutting herself. Her parents sent her to therapy, but unfortunately it didn't seem to help. After writing her parents notes apologizing for what she was about to do, Rosaline hung herself. After a few days she was taken off life-support.

Aina Adewunmi

When starting a new school, it can be challenging for any young person. It can even worse when you encounter bullying at that new school. Well, that is what happened to Aina Adewunmi.

Aina was able to meet some friends, and was added to a group chat. Soon after being added, she noticed that some of the conversations exhibited racial undertones. After letting the group know that this was not okay, one particular young man continued his racist remarks. Once his remarks continued she decided to end their friendship.

After severing her friendship, she soon came across a photo of herself, taken without her knowledge, with a noose drawn around her neck. Angry and afraid, she reported it immediately to the school's principal. The young man and a few of his friends were suspended for the remainder of the school year.

As I mentioned before, unfortunately, there are several stories/cases on bullying you can find simply by using your favorite internet search engine. They represent all bullying types, and affect people from every gender, race, religion and nationality. No one is exempt from bullying. Even though bullying has been around for years, it has changed dramatically, and is getting worse.

Social media has played a major role in bullying over the past few years. In the next chapter we will explore the role of social media and bullying.

Chapter Three

Reflection

1. Did you notice any differences in bullying between the different generations? If so, what were they?

2. Did your child experience bullying during the years of 2001- present? If so, how did they handle it?

Chapter Four

The Social

Media Effect

<u>Ask Yourself.......</u>

1. How familiar are you with Social Media?

2. What Social Media Applications do you use?

3. Do you have access to your child's Social Media?

4. What does going viral mean?

Social Media was first recognized in 1997 with a site called Six Degrees. Six Degrees, as well as some of the other social media sites such as Myspace, Facebook and LinkedIn, were created to provide a circle where old and new friends could come together and communicate. Each became popular in its own individual way and have/had millions of users.

With any good thing there can also be some cause for concern. Social Media has given bullies a new and improved way to bully people. It helped create a new category for bullying called cyberbullying. Of course, this was never the intention of the internet or social media. Unfortunately, this type of behavior ran and continues to run rampant. More than likely it will get worse before it gets better.

Statistics on Cyberbullying

- Almost 34% of students acknowledged they have been cyberbullied.

- 87% of today's youth have witnessed cyberbullying.

- 15% of surveyed students admit to cyberbullying others.

- Girls tend to favor social media outlets like Snapchat or Instagram, while boys often interact over gaming consoles.

- Male cyberbullies often post hurtful photos or videos.

- 50% of youth have been involved in an argument because of something posted on social media.

Teen Safe (October 4, 2016) Cyberbullying Facts and Statistics https://www.teensafe.com/blog/cyber-bullying-facts-and-statistics/

How Social Media Fueled Cyberbullying

Social media allows people to bully and harass their targets from behind a computer screen. Here they can, if only for a moment, say or do, whatever they want with no immediate consequences. It is also allowing them to sometimes do it anonymously. When you encounter a bully in-person, you have an easier path to follow when you attempt to stop it. When the bullying is online, there are several factors that can make it seem like an impossible barrier to get over. Here are some of the ways it can present a challenge.

Bullying with and without a face

There are supposed to be rules that people abide by when using social media apps, but this is not always the case. People find a way to work around these "so-called" rules. When work-around ways are found it allows bullies multiple ways to target their victims.

One of the flaws with social media is the ability to create multiple profiles. If a person is banned from a social media site, all they have to do is create another profile and request the same friends all over again. In the snap of a finger, they have another profile to post from. One gets banned or suspended, and they switch right over to their back up, and continue their harassment.

It also allows people to create completely anonymous profiles. With social media, a person can be anyone they want. The TV show, *Catfish,* made this abundantly clear to me. When I first watched the show I remember thinking there was no way this show could be real. With all of the available options to communicate with others face-to-face via phone applications, and/or social media, I thought there's no way this could happen. Until I had a conversation with a friend who told me she had a family member that does this all the time. This person led others to believe he is someone else. I remember being stunned, thinking how could this be so? Soon after learning this, I encountered several people who have had similar experiences. This was a bigger issue than I'd imagined.

If the internet and social media allow ways for people to catfish those seeking love and friendship, it can also be used as another avenue to bully. People create "ghost-profiles" to do their dirty work. They can harass, stalk and bully people without anyone knowing who they really are. If there are moderators to the social media site, they can suspend the bully's profile. However, if the bully is relentless, they can just create a new profile and pick up right where they left off. There are some sites that have no moderators to regulate the sites; therefore no one can intervene if needed.

Leaves a forever trail

Using these sites make people who use them "Googleable." This is a word I made up to describe the ability to use an internet search engine to find information on any of us. Anything we post, and anything that has ever been written about us, can be found online.

Pictures and videos that are meant only for family and friends can quickly "go viral", putting them in the hands of the wrong people. For instance, a young man is hanging with his friends who record him yelling racially insensitive remarks to a fellow classmate. Or, maybe a young lady gets asked by a boy she likes to send him a racy photo of her, just for him. Then when he receives it, he sends the picture to his friend, and then that friend sends   it to another friend, and so on and so forth. The next thing you know, everyone in the school has seen and has a copy of her photo and they are using it to bully and harass her.

These are all things young people may have done when they were young, but material shared over the internet, and/or text message, leaves a virtual fingerprint that can potentially follow them forever. In either scenario, these are situations I am sure they would like to forget and leave in the past. However, the internet is undefeated when it comes to finding long-lost "skeletons" people want to stay buried. These pictures can come back to haunt them and affect future employment, education opportunities and other favorable possibilities due to thing they did in their youth. It won't matter if they have changed and no longer do these things. Unfortunately, the focus will be placed on their past transgressions.

Is this practice fair? Maybe it is, or maybe it is not. Sadly, this is currently happening to a lot of youth and young adults, and affecting them profoundly.

Chapter Four

<u>Reflection</u>

1. Google yourself. Did you find any information good or bad about yourself? If so, what did you find?

2. How would your life and social status be affected today if some of your past transgressions were brought were exposed?

Chapter Five

Are You Kids

Prepared To

Fight Back?

<u>Ask Yourself….</u>

1. Were you ever bullied as a child?

2. In your adolescent years, how were you told bullies needed to be handled?

3. Did you ever fight a bully when you were a child? If so, how did it turn out?

I will never forget the day I found footage of a mother forcing her son to fight a "supposed bully". She stated several times during the video that her son was going to become a man that day. She yelled and screamed demanding her son fight the other little boy. She was determined that he was going to fight. I could tell by looking at her son that he was very uncomfortable and afraid of the other kid. I wondered if her son was even prepared to fight this little boy, or anyone else for that matter. I would soon have my answer.

After much pressure from his mother, he reluctantly engaged in a fight with the other young man. It was painfully obvious this child was not as experienced in fighting as the other kid. So much so that, in no time, the other little boy was on top pounding him. Eventually, his mother stepped in and pulled the boy off of her son. Most people would think the mother would have let it end there, that was not the case. While her son was screaming that he no longer wanted to fight, she continued to yell at him to continue the fight. Oh! I forgot to mention that there was a crowd around "egging" the fight on and of course there was someone there recording the entire thing. Needless to say this was difficultto watch.

All sorts of emotions ran through me as I was watching this video. I was horrified! I have shared this video several times during my bullying workshops, and every participant shared my same feeling. Now, the twist to this situation was that before I showed this each and every one of the participants stated that they had told their children to do the same thing this mother told her son. They all stated that the mother in the video had gone too far and was out of line. I asked them to explain the difference between what she did and what they stated earlier? I believe that viewing what this behavior actually looks like was eye-opening for most. It caused them to think differently.

It is totally understandable to tell your child that if someone hits them they should hit them back. With that being said, I have the following questions for you. "Will they be prepared to deal with the possible consequences that may come with hitting their bully back?" "What happens if they attempt to fight back and their bully still over-powers them?" "What would they do then?"

I am not telling you that your child shouldn't let anyone just hit them and do nothing about it. My point is, please make sure your child is able to defend themselves before you tell them to fight back. If they cannot defend themselves they run the risk of making the situation worse.

Time and time again, I hear parents say to their children (whether in front of me or told via their child), "If anyone hits you, you hit them back!" "Either you are going to go back and fight them, or you are going to have to fight me!" These statements, and statements like these, anger me. I always fire back with, "How do you know your kid can fight?" There have been some parents that say they have prepared their child to defend themselves, but a majority of the time my question is met with silence. My follow-up question is always, "Why would you send your child into this situation and they are not prepared to defend themselves?"

Telling your child to stand up for themselves is perfectly fine. My only request is that you consider the following:

1. Have a conversation with your child to see where they are mentally and emotionally.

2. Ask them how comfortable they are with fighting back.

3. Ask them what they need from you.

Have a conversation with your child to see where they are mentally and emotionally.

Being bullied is very emotional and affects your child mentally. If they are coming to you, they are looking for your support. Allow them to be transparent and feel comfortable with telling you how they are feeling. They may ask for space and this is okay. Space doesn't necessarily mean that you leave them alone to deal with the issue, but grant space for them to process what has happened to them. Some children recover a lot faster than others, and some may take a little longer. Everyone's process is different and sometimes the process may include therapy. Do whatever it takes to make sure they are recovering from their experience. Trauma as a result of bullying left unresolved can lead to serious and lasting problems.

Ask them comfortable they are with fighting back?

I remember conducting a bullying workshop for parents and having an intense conversation on this topic. While talking to my class about simply telling your child to fight back this gentleman raised his hand. When I acknowledged him he stated, "My son better not come in my house talking about somebody is bullying him! Either he is going to have to fight me, or he is going back out there to fight that bully." I asked him, "What if there is more than one person out there he would have to fight?" His response was, "Well he's gotta learn some time." Then another woman in the class chimed in and said, "Yeah, that's what we used to do when we were coming up I kept going back and forth with this father trying to explain that things are not like they used to be. In the present day, one-on-one fights are few and far between, and he needed to understand this. I remember looking at his son who was seated beside him with his head hanging down. He never said a word, he just sat there. My heart went out to him. I wondered what he was thinking and how he felt about what his father was saying. I also curious if after hearing what his dad has said, if he would feel comfortable telling his father if he was ever bullied. I wish I would have pulled him to the side asked him.

After going back and forth with this father and others in the workshop I decided we could all just agree to disagree, and table the conversation for the moment. Several years after this workshop, I still remember that young man's face. I wish I would have been in the state of mind to ask his father this very important question. "Have you taught your son how to defend himself?" "Maybe he did, and then again maybe he didn't, but it was never addressed during our conversation. His father mentioned that he needed to learn, but is it always necessary, or the only way, to learn how do something by the sink or swim method? Is it possible to ask if he feels like he is able to go out and defend himself? Is it also possible to place him in a program, or at least have a conversation with his son?

show him how to defend himself? What if his son goes out there unprepared and gets hurt? What does that aftermath look like? How do you help your child move past that possible defeat? These are questions I think **some** parents fail to think about.

I may be over reacting, but what if I am not? It is it is worth having a conversation with your child to find out. I believe that just throwing your child in to the fire without preparing them (if possible) is irresponsible. Assuming that your child will automatically be prepared for this with a little push can be dangerous and can be detrimental to your relationship with your child. It could cause your child to feel like they cannot come to you about their bullying situation. They may feel like you will force them into a situation without them being ready. Before you possibly send your child go fight their bully without

verifying they are prepared for it, , ask them first.

Ask them what they need from you.

Parents are their children's protectors. If they are

being hurt, parents swing in to action to protect their child

at all cost. This is great, but oftentimes there is one thing

missing from the equation. Parents may never stop to ask

what their child needs from them.

Being there for your child and protecting your child is

definitely what your child needs, just consider including

them in the process or allowing them to try to fix the

problem on their own first. Try to look at it like this. Do

you remember when your child wanted to learn to do something new?

A mother told me a story once about her daughter. Her daughter started school and needed to wear button up shirts. She had worn button up shirts before, but the mother buttoned them up for her. One day, the daughter decided that she wanted to button up her own shirts from now on. I am sure her daughter had watched her previously and wanted to try to do it by herself. When her mother allowed her to try for herself, she sometimes needed assistance but eventually she learned to do it all by herself. Her mom was there for oversight, but she did it on her own.

The moral to this story is, sometimes they would like to at least be given the option to at least try to solve their problem and have your full support as well. Maybe they can handle it by themselves and maybe they can't, but at least give them the option. Let them know you are there to support them and you are ready to step in if necessary. I know this maybe a difficult thing to do but, it may be a necessary step in assisting your child through this process. These steps can be essential in finding the most effective way to help your child.

Chapter 5

<u>Reflection</u>

1. Have you ever asked your child how they would react if they were ever bullied? Why or why not?

2. Have you ever taught or placed your child in a program to possible teach them self-defense? Why or why not?

3. After reading this chapter, would you handle anything differently if your child were ever in this situation? Why or why not?

Chapter Six

Why Won't My Child Talk Me?

<u>Ask Yourself….</u>

1. If your child was being bullied, do you feel comfortable saying that your child would tell you?

2. If you were bullied as a child, did you immediately tell your parents?

3. What do you think would keep your child from telling you they have been bullied?

Parents sometimes wonder why it may take so long for their kids to talk to them about their bullying problem or they are baffled as to why their kids didn't tell them that they are being bullied. Many parents expressed that they have an open relationship with their children and struggle to understand why they didn't come to them.

I have had the opportunity to talk to thousands of students to ask them these very questions. Their responses varied some, but there responses were always reflected back to these same three categories. The categories are as follows:

<u>They are afraid of how you will react:</u>

Once while I was out in the community conducting a bullying workshop, a local news station was there to do a story on our Bullying workshop we were offering. There is a part of the workshop where we explore possible reasons why kids may not tell their parents they are being bullied. There was one young man's statement that will always stick with me and I use it often till this day.

While we were exploring different reasons why kids don't tell their parents, this young man raised his hand and wanted to share a story. He went on to explain why he would never tell his mother he was being bullied. The news story quoted him saying "My mom would be coming all up to the school going all off on everybody!" Thank God for editing because what he actually said was "My momma is crazy! She would be coming all up to the school going off on everybody and embarrassing me!"

I am not sure if his original statement would have embarrassed or disturbed his mother, but his statement spoke volumes to me.

When someone is being bullied not only is it hurtful it is also embarrassing. Oftentimes it can make the situation worse if parents and or siblings come up to the school (or where the bullying occurs) causing a big scene. Let me ask you this this. When you were in school and someone's mom came up to the school because their child was in trouble. Do you remember what some of the other kids would do? "Oooh who's momma is that?" "You are gonna get it!" Has this ever happened to you or someone close to you? If so, how did that make you, or them, feel? No one wants to be embarrassed. As a matter of fact, **most** really would prefer that nobody know. If your kids feel that you will your actions may bring more humiliation chances are they will not confide in you and tell you what they may be going through.

They also could be afraid that you will do nothing or minimize their situation. They could possibly be worried that you will say things like: "Honey they are just being kids. Don't worry about it." Or you may say something like "Don't be so sensitive all the time."

Parents, please do not take this information as a shot at you personally or your individual parenting style. No one is claiming not to understand or trying to condemn a parent who may do this. Kids who may feel like this want their parents to acknowledge that there is indeed a problem and they may need your help. Dealing with bullying is very difficult and we must make sure we are helping our kids to the best of our abilities and not add more hurt and frustration to an already difficult situation.

<u>They don't want to be known as a snitch</u>

We have heard the saying "Snitches get snitches" or sayings related to telling on others. Kids hear these things all around them and we wonder why they may not tell you when something is going on with them. Sometimes unintentionally parents can also reinforce the" no snitching" behavior.

I know some of you are read my last sentence and you may be a little put off by my statement. Please give me a minute to explain. Have you ever told your child to "Stop being a tattle-tail!"? Or maybe told them to "Stop telling so much!"? Then when something bad does happen or someone does something to them and they say nothing. Does any of this sound familiar? I am not trying to point fingers, but I am trying to draw a parallel between the two. There are times where telling or getting help are imperative. To understand the difference between the two sometimes clarification is needed.

They feel afraid, powerless and ashamed

I am afraid of dogs. This is not something I am very proud of but it is true. I sometimes hesitate telling people that I have this fear because I fear how I will be treated. Many times I feel like my fears have been minimized and dismissed as being absurd. For years I have avoided homes of friends and family if they had pets, especially if they were kept in the house. Let me explain my fear.

I have always had a afraid of dogs. On top of that fear as little girl, I was attacked by a dog. It wasn't a real big dog but never the less, I was attacked. That incident combined with a pre-existing fear snowballed into an even bigger fear.

One evening I was getting out of my car to walk into my house. One of my neighbors was outside with their dog that was not on a leash. I am trying to conquer my fear of dogs, so I got out of my car and proceeded to walk to my house. As I was walking with an arm full of items, I dropped an item on the ground. This got the attention of the dog and it turns and starts charges towards me. I hear the dog's owner call the dog's name to stop but the dog continued to charge me. I remember standing there with nowhere to go. My car was now locked, I hadn't reached my front door yet so it was shut and locked as well I remember yelling "Oh My God!" as the dog got closer and closer. By the Grace of God, the dog turned back less than two feet away from me. The owner yelled out to me "Oh she won't hurt you." That was no comfort to me at all. I was angry we he would even said that to me.

Later that evening, I decided to share my experience on Facebook. Although, most comments were supportive, I received a few laughing emojis and some other dismissive comments. One comment stuck out more than the others. A high school friend made a comment with a huge line of laughing emojis. I replied and asked her what was so funny. Her response alluded to the fact that dogs were our friends and it was funny to her that I was afraid. Her comments about my fear really angered me. It felt like I was being shamed for being afraid. I felt she had very little empathy for my feelings. Through the years I have felt like this too many times to count.

I know you are wondering what my story has to do with kids being afraid to tell their parents about them being bullied. The same way I am afraid of dogs it the same way they are afraid of their bullies. The same way I adjusted where I go or left a place because of a presence of a dog is the same way they duck and dodge their bullies. I hesitate to tell others about my fear of dogs because it is minimized and this is the same they hesitate to tell others about their fears on being afraid of their They are afraid they will be told to toughen up or referred to as weak. Rather than to ask for help, they will keep silent and hope that eventually the bullying will stop on its own. Sometimes this may work and unfortunately sometimes it doesn't.

Bullying is embarrassing and can be overwhelming thing to deal with. Worrying about how you may handle the situation can be overwhelming as well. With your reassurance and help, they can move past their fears and start communication with you to find a solution to their bullying issues.

Chapter 6

<u>Reflection</u>

1. If you felt like your child was dealing with a problem but hasn't told to you about it, how would you go about getting them to talk to you about it?

2. If you found out your child was being bullied, what would be the first thing you would do?

3. How would you explain the difference between when being a "tattletale" or "snitch" is appropriate and not appropriate?

Chapter Seven

Are You Part Of The Problem?

<u>Ask Yourself……</u>

1. How do you feel about videoing the discipline your child (ren) and placing it on social media?

2. Have you ever recorded yourself when are disciplining your child (ren)?

I realize that parents are looking to find ways that will impact their children the most when disciplining them. Although I believe parents are doing what they think is the best thing for their children, but in the process, they may be causing my harm than good. I honestly believe that no parent that loves their child would ever intentionally hurt or potentially put their child in a compromising position. Unfortunately when they are trying to combine social media and "old school discipline" often can be counter-productive.

The Internet Is Forever!

When we were younger, usually when it came to discipline, what happened in the home stayed in the home. It was more accepted to spank or whip your children when there was a need for discipline. We also didn't have phones with video capabilities or social media to broadcast everything. We must continue to remind ourselves that times have changed. What you do today on social media can and affect you and your child for the rest of their lives. Please take a look at these examples with an open mind and open heart.

Facebook Live

In mid-2016, a video surfaced on social media of a mother severely beating her 16 year old daughter with her bare hands. This apparently all started because her daughter posted a picture of herself in a towel with her boyfriend on social media. Once her mother found about this photo, it was all downhill after that.

All this mother could think about was all she has sacrificed for both of her daughters and how she didn't raise her do things like this. She knew she wanted to punish her daughter, but how. She wanted to make sure to leave a serious impression on her daughter to make sure she would never do anything like this again. She decided that she would show her daughter's punishment on the same social media format where she shared the riske' photo She got her younger daughter use the social media's live option to showcase the punishment.

She punched her daughter in the face and on various parts of her body. This beating went on for what seemed like forever. While the mother was hitting her daughter, she calls her names like "Thot' (slang for that hoe over there) constantly throughout the ordeal. Her daughter screamed and cried telling her mother she was sorry. She begged her mother not to hit her anymore. She attempted to say whatever her mother wanted to hear to try to satisfy her questions and stop hitting her. Once she finally finished "punishing "her daughter she left her live video with a message for everyone who was watching. She was taking over her daughter's page from now on. She said she would not be disrespected and she wanted this video to become viral. She also said there would be more to come.

Of course, this video went viral as her mother wanted. There was a mix of supporters of the mother and others who disagreed with her actions. There were some people that were so upset that they alerted child protective services as well as their local police department. They were horrified at what they were witnessing and thought the authorities needed to be involved. Others were very vocal and believed that everyone else needed to mind their own business. They believed that this woman was doing what she needed to teach her daughter what she did was unacceptable. They thought that the mother did what she had to do and that if more parents did their kids that way more kids wouldn't act that way. This mother never faced any official charges, but she did have an investigation done on her and her family. Her daughter was removed temporarily for her custody.

Whatever side of the fence you are on, it is evident that this video left an impression on everyone who watched it. It made so much of an impact that this story eventually made several news outlets and eventually CNN.

<u>Snapchat</u>

In early December, I was strolling down my timeline and saw a video of a father and daughter. This video stuck out to me for a variety of reasons. As I pushed play, I noticed that the father was recording a recording he did from Snapchat. Apparently, his teen daughter had a boyfriend and was talking about how she was down for him in a video on this social media site. This did not sit well with the father. He decided to punish his daughter on the social media app that she recorded her message on. After berating her saying that she had no business with a boyfriend and among other hurtful things. Then he took a pause from publicly shaming his daughter, he told her to kneel in front of the couch. While she was in front of the couch, he took out his belt and proceeded to strike his daughter 51 times.

After he finished giving her lashing, he instructed her to take a seat in on a kitchen stool. He was still talking about her having a boyfriend and what she said about him on Snapchat. Then he moved to the next phase of his discipline. He took a pair of clippers and began to cut his entire daughter's hair off. He shaved her completely bald. When he finished, he instructed her to look at the camera so everyone watching could see her. I am not sure who was filming this event, but I can only imagine what was going through this person's mind as they were a firsthand witness to punishment. Her eyes were filled with tears; she looked into the camera to show the world what her father had done to her.

This sent shockwaves throughout social media. Again, the comments were divided on whether the father went too far with his punishment. I don't have much information on what happened with this young lady and her father. There was rumor that he was arrested for what he did, but I cannot confirm or deny that report.

Unintentional Celebrity

A mother had reached her wit's end with her son getting in trouble. He had a problem with taking things that do not belong to him. He also had a habit of lying and he had been arrested a quite few times. He had gone through the court process and still nothing worked. She felt she needed to do something drastic to reach her son.

She decided to make her son wear a large sign saying, "I lie, I steal, I sell drugs and I don't follow the law" and had him to stand on a local street corner. She never posted her son on social media nor did she take any pictures of her son on this corner.

Motorist rode by this woman and her son and some were disturbed by what she was doing. They were so disturbed about what they saw, they called police. Police came by and to investigate what was going on. When the police came to investigate the situation, so did their local T.V. Station.

While this mother is being interviewed, she shares the problems she has been having with her 14 year old son. She said he had been to court and been on probation and nothing has seemed to work. She said she was willing to do whatever she needed to do to save her son. While they were interviewing the mother, they also took several shots of her son and did not attempt to blur his face.

Police concluded that even though this method was unconventional, it was not illegal. No charges were brought against this mother.

There are several stories I could have shared and believe me there are many. I searched my mind to try to share the ones that could possibly make the biggest impact. While recalling these stories, I tried to remain neutral and not try to sway you the reader in any direction. I have to admit that was a struggle. A couple of these stories ripped my heart out while watching them.

My take on these stories are simple. Something you post has the potential to be accessible online forever. These young ladies and young man are young and I am sure they will go on to do wonderful and promising things with their lives. Here is the catch to that. Sadly, since their parents decided to share their child's name and offense to the entire world, anyone who wants to find these stories can do a google search and find them. When they get older and move on to bigger and better things, these episodes of their lives could always come back to haunt them. Enemies could try use information to tarnish their reputations. One parent's intent was not to include posting her story on any type of social media like the other two parents. However, when she conducted her son's punishment in public, she too contributed to her son being plastered all over the news and social media.

Again, I honestly believe when these parents did these things they had no idea their stories would grow to this viral state they did. I believe in their minds, they were ultimately doing what they thought they needed to do to make the punishment impactful to their child. Whether you believe they were right or wrong, that is your opinion and that is to be respected. The only thing I want parents to realize is how what they do today can and will affect their children in the years to come. You have to ask yourselves, is this really what you wanted to accomplish? You are the only one who can answer that question. Whatever your answer is, I hope you consider these stories before you make your final decision.

Chapter 7

Reflection

1. Will these stories cause you to think twice before using social media to disciplining your child? Why or why not?

2. If you were to see a child being disciplined and/or abused on social media by a parent, would you report it? Why or why not?

3. When thinking about the kids in these stories, what are some of the after effects their kids may endure?

Chapter 8

Where Do We Go From Here?

Where Do We Do Now?

I am often asked by parents what they could do to help their child when and if they are being bullied. I wish I had a fix all answer that could take this bullying issue away for good, but I don't. However, I do have some advice and some steps that I believe will be helpful if your child is ever in this situation.

Step 1: Look for warning signs

- Has unexplained cuts, bruises, and scratches

- Seems afraid of going to school, walking to and from school, riding the school bus, or taking part in organized activities with peers (such as clubs)

- Has lost interest in school work or suddenly begins to do poorly in school

- Appears sad, moody, teary, or depressed when he or she comes home from school

- Complains frequently of headaches, stomach aches, or other physical ailments

- Was once very social and then turns to isolation

It there is an issue with bullying:

- **Determine the source of the bullying**. Find out the Who, What, and Where. Please do not gather this information to go and confront another child unless absolutely necessary. You will look like a bully to someone else's child.

- **Start collecting evidence.** The more evidence you have to support claims that your child is being bullied, the better. Keep record of pictures, bruises, incidences dates, times and places bullying may have taken place. Also, take screen shots of online harassment,

- **If your child has to defend themselves, please prepare them for it.** There may become a time where your child may need to defend themselves. Unless you know your child can defend themselves, please don't assume that they can. Explore different possibilities that could prepare them for this time if it comes.

- **Stay calm.** I know this can be a very hard thing to do when someone is hurting your child. Your child is upset and it is hard to see your child in that state. The main focus is to get the issue resolved for your child as quickly as possible. We have to remember is that someone has to remain calm to make sure the problem comes to an acceptable conclusion. If you are upset, and out of control and reflecting that emotion onto to others can be counterproductive.

- **Ask your child what they need from you.** Parents are protectors of their families. If your child is being hurt, parents want to fix it immediately. Sometimes, in the haste to fix the problem for them, they are never asked what help they actually need. Yes you are their parent and you know what is best for them, however include your child in the solution. Remember this is an uncomfortable time for your child and that needs to be acknowledged. You don't want them to shut down and not communicate with you anymore so keep them in the loop when possible.

- **Please do not minimize their experience.** As I have mentioned before, being bullied is a hurtful, embarrassing and uncomfortable situation. It takes a lot for anyone to admit they have been bullied and to ask for help. If they are met with statements such as: "Kids are just being kids.", "Kids are just mean sometimes," or "Maybe you just need to toughen up a little." can be very detrimental. It can come off as dismissive and make your child second guess sharing their experience again. They are coming to you because they your assistance and realize they cannot handle it on their own. Listen to them and help them sort through this uneasy situation to help them come to a solution.

If the bullying occurs at school

- **Know your child's school policy on bullying**. If they do not have one, they should. Be willing to volunteer and work with school personnel to create one.

- **Follow the chain of protocol**. Example: If it happens in a teacher's class, notify the teacher. If that doesn't stop it, go to the vice principle or school resource officer. Next the principal. If nothing changes, be prepared to take the problem to the school board and or the police to file a complaint. Most parents are reluctant to press charges on another child and hopefully it will not get to this point. If it does, you cannot be slow to act. Your child is depending on you and if it calls for the police to be involved you have to do it.

- **Be open to having a conversation with the parents of the bully.** I would recommend attempting to resolve bullying issues with the other parents if possible. In order for this to work, everyone has to have an open mind and only give fact-based and evidence-based accusations. Both sides have to commit to being fair and reasonable. If these conditions and terms cannot be agreed upon beforehand, I recommend bringing in a neutral party to mediate.

• **Get involved at your child's school.** Keep in close contact with your child's teachers and other school staff. Not only when there is something wrong, but when things are going well also. It is important to keep those lines of communication open. Attend PTA meetings and any other school meetings whenever possible. Stay informed of the happenings in your child's school. I also recommend random visits and sometimes unannounced visits. This is not to catch schools in a so called "gotcha moment" but to stay informed with daily activities in your child's school. It will give a clear synopsis of what could possibly be regular day –to- day operations when guests are not expected.

If the bullying occurs outside of school

- **Tell your child to avoid walking off by themselves**. Many times bullying takes place when the bullied is by themselves. Bullies take advantage of this situation because the bullied is in a vulnerable state. Bullies may take this time to show off in front of their friends at your child's expense. This also increases the likelihood that your child may be at risk of being outnumbered and possible being jumped. If they are not able to have someone with them at all times, you may want to look at alternate routes your child may need to take in order to be less vulnerable.

- **If the bullying takes place online, do not respond to it.** When you start to gather evidence it does not seem like it is two people arguing instead of your child being bullied. I know this may be hard to do, but not responding will be crucial to proving your case.

- **Be prepared in case you have to involve law enforcement.** When bullying happens in and around school it may be a little easier when reporting incidences and seeking help. When it happens outside of the schools proximity, the process gets a little more rigid. Police and maybe even lawyer may need to be involved. When pressing charges or filing a complaint court may be inevitable. Evidence is a must and if you don't have any evidence you will more than likely lose your case.

- **Know the laws in your state.** If you have to go through all of the time and expense of preparing a case, it helps to know the law in your state. Unfortunately the law has lagged behind in passing laws and creating legislature in regards to bullying and cyberbullying. Due to the increase and severity of bullying, lawmakers are realizing the need to pay closer attention to this issue. If your state does not have any laws, or if they are very broad, you may be the person to assist with this change. Sometimes we wait for something bad to happen or for someone else to lead the charge. Don't be afraid to step up and be that person to lead the charge.

I really wish that I had a solution to end bullying, but I don't. However, I do believe that there are things that we do to help curb some of the behavior. If we can all agree to work together and stop condoning and minimizing bullying type behaviors.

You cannot change what you don't acknowledge. We must acknowledge that bullying is bigger than kids just being kids. We have to realize that with different generations there comes change. With all of the changes in technology and access bullying has gotten worse. We cannot continue to tell our children to handle bullying the same we did when we were children. We have to evolve, have conversations and work together to effectively figure out how to best help our children deal with this issue.

Bonus

Resources and

Information

Risk Factors That Your Child May Be or Become A Bully

- ☐ A lack of unintentional involvement on the part of parents

- ☐ Lack of clear boundaries for children's behavior

- ☐ Bullying incidences at school

- ☐ Could be bullied by older or younger siblings

- ☐ Complains frequently of headaches, stomach aches, or other physical ailments

Ways To Deter Your Child From Being A Bully

- ➢ Recognize that yes; it could be your child that is being a bully.

- ➢ Talk to your child about his/her bullying behavior. Try to pinpoint the cause of this behavior.

- ➢ Inform your child on how bullying affects the victim

- ➢ Establish ground rules and consequences for your child to follow regarding their behavior toward others and be consistent

- ➢ Work together with your child and his/her school counselor.

- ➢ Get them involved in positive activities.

- ➢ Utilize professional counseling if needed.

Possible Consequences To Irresponsible Social Media Use

☐ Youth may endanger themselves by not understanding the public and/or viral possibilities on social networking sites.

➢ Using social media can harm students' chances for college admissions.

☐ In appropriate social media use can harm job stability and employment prospects.

☐ Un-safe challenges or online activity can encourage poor decision making.

☐ Youth can enter into dangerous situations and/or relationships

☐ Once something is put out on the internet, you can never permanently delete it

Movies To Watch

Bully, by Lee Hirsch

Bully is an unflinching look at how bullying has touched five kids and their families, revealing a problem inspired by a true story.

Cyberbully, ABC Family Films

A teenager is subjected to a campaign of bullying by classmates through a social networking site.

Girl Fight, Lifetime Movies

Inspired by a true story, a telling the tale of a 16-year-old high school student whose life begins a downward spiral when she is brutally assaulted by her former friends.

13 Reasons Why, Netflix Movies

The series revolves around seventeen year old high school student, his deceased female friend who has committed suicide after failing to cope with the culture, gossip and lack of support from her friends and her school.

<u>Things you can do to better prepare your</u>

<u>kids</u>

- Self-defense class
- Counseling
- Conflict resolutions skills

Free Useful Apps and Websites for Parents

- **Common Sense Media**: An information hub that allows families make smart media choices. They offer the largest, most trusted library of independent age-based and educational ratings and reviews for movies, games, apps, TV shows, websites, books, and music.

- **Life 360**: This app runs on your mobile device to allow you to view your family members on a map, communicate with them, their GPS location, receive alerts when your loved ones arrive at home, school or work and so much more.

- **OurPact:** This app teaches responsible and safe digital use with tools that enable parents to set time limits on smartphone use, create schedules, block apps and internet access, and even reward your teens with extra time when and if you see fit.

Monica McLaurine, a Bullying expert and she is a well-known social media safety consultant. While presenting at several Bullying Conferences throughout the United States, Monica has been fortunate to empower and educate people of all ages on bullying and its effects. She is very passionate and is dedicated to giving bullying survivors a voice. Her first book offering was *Becoming Comfortable in My Own Skin: The Journey to Loving Me* and she is excited to present her second book *I Told My Kid To Fight Back: Examining Generational Differences Between Yesterday and Today.*

A native is a native of Nashville, Tennessee. Monica has also has a Bachelor's degree in Criminal Justice, from the University of Tennessee at Chattanooga. In her spare time, Monica loves to spend time with family and friends, travel, exercise and shop.

www.ingramcontent.com/pod-product-compliance
Lightning Source LLC
LaVergne TN
LVHW051352080426
835509LV00020BB/3394